YANKEE DAWG YOU DIE

BY PHILIP KAN GOTANDA

★

DRAMATISTS
PLAY SERVICE
INC.

YANKEE DAWG YOU DIE
Copyright © 1991, Philip Kan Gotanda

All Rights Reserved

SPECIAL NOTE

SPECIAL NOTE ON SONGS AND RECORDINGS

YANKEE DAWG YOU DIE was presented by Playwrights Horizons (Andre Bishop, Artistic Director) in New York City, in April, 1989. It was directed by Sharon Ott; the set design was by Kent Dorsey; the costume design was by Jess Goldstein; the lighting design was by Dan Kotlowitz; the music and sound design was by Stephen LeGrand and Eric Drew Feldman; the production stage manager was Robin Rumpf and the production manager was Carl Mulert. The cast was as follows:

VINCENT CHANG ....Sab Shimono
BRADLEY YAMASHITA ....Stan Egi

YANKEE DAWG YOU DIE received its world premiere at the Berkeley Repertory Theatre (Sharon Ott, Artistic Director; Mitzi Sales, Managing Director) in Berkeley, California, in February, 1988. The production was subsequently moved to the Los Angeles Theatre Center in May of 1988. It was directed by Sharon Ott; the set and lighting design was by Kent Dorsey; the costume design was by Lydia Tanji; the sound design was by James LeBrecht; original music was by Stephen LeGrand and Eric Drew Feldman; the assistant director was Phyllis S. K. Look and the stage manager was Michael Suenkel. In the Los Angeles Theatre Center production, the co-lighting designer was Douglas Smith. The cast was as follows:

VINCENT CHANG ....Sab Shimono
BRADLEY YAMASHITA ....Kelvin Han Yee

CHARACTERS

VINCENT CHANG: Actor. Mid to late 60's. Former hoofer.

BRADLEY YAMASHITA: Actor. Mid to late 20's.

SET

Minimal with a hint of fragmentation and distortion of perspective to allow for a subtle dream-like quality. Upstage, high-tech shoji screens for title and visual projections. Set should allow for a certain fluidity of movement. Allow for lights to be integral in scene transitions. Suggested colors — black with red accents.

LIGHTING

Fluid. Interludes should use cross-fades. Dream sequences might experiment with color and shafts of light cutting at askew angles, film-noirish.

MUSIC

Minimal instrumentation. Classical in feel.

YANKEE DAWG YOU DIE

INTRODUCTION

Darkness. Filmic music score enters. Then, on the projection screens upstage we see emblazoned the following titles:

"[Name of Producing Theatre] PRESENTS..."

"VINCENT CHANG..."

Vincent lit in pool of light, staring pensively into the dark-ness. The music dips and we hear the faint beating of a heart. A hint of blood red washes over Vincent as he lightly touches his breast near his heart area. Fade to black.

"AND INTRODUCING..."

"BRADLEY YAMASHITA"

Bradley lit in pool of light. Restless, shifting his weight back and forth on his feet. The music dips and we hear the light rustling of large wings. As he looks skyward, a large shadow passes over head. Fade to black.

"IN..."

"YANKEE DAWG YOU DIE..."

The entire theater — stage as well as audience area — is gradually inundated in an ocean of stars. Hold for a mo-ment, then a slow fade to black.

INTERLUDE 1

Lights come up. Vincent portraying a "Jap soldier." Lighting creates the mood of an old 40's black and white movie. Thick Coke-bottle glasses, holding a gun. Acts in an exaggerated, stereotypic — almost cartoonish manner.

Sergeant Moto pretends to be falling asleep while guarding American prisoners. The snake-like lids of his slanty eyes drooping into a feigned slumber. Suddenly Moto's eyes spitting hates and bile, flash open, catching the American prisoners in the midst of their escape plans.

VINCENT. *(As Moto.)* You stupid American G.I. I know you try and escape. You think you can pull my leg. I speakee your language. I graduate UCLA, Class of '34. I drive big American car with big-chested American blond sitting next to ... Heh? No, no, no, not "dirty floor." Floor clean. Class of '34. No, no, not "dirty floor." Floor clean. Just clean this morning. 34. No, no, not "dirty floor." Listen carefully. Watch my lips. *(He moves his lips but the words are not synched with them ala poorly-dubbed Japanese monster movie.)* 34. 34! 34!!! *(Pause. Return to synched speaking.)* What is wrong with you? You sickee in the head? What the hell is wrong with you? Why can't you hear what I'm saying? Why can't you see me as I really am? *(Vincent as Sergeant Moto dims to darkness.)*

End of Interlude

ACT I

Scene One

"YOU LOOKED LIKE A FUCKING CHIMPANZEE"

Night. Party. House in Hollywood Hills. Vincent Chang, a youthful, silver-maned man, in his late 60's, stands on the back terrace balcony sipping on a glass of red wine. Stares into the night air. Bradley Yamashita, 27, pokes his head out from the party and notices Vincent. Stops, losing his nerve. Changes his mind again and moves out on the terrace next to Vincent. Bradley holds a cup of club soda.

Silence. Vincent notices Bradley, Bradley smiles, Vincent nods. Silence. They both sip on their drinks.

BRADLEY.   Hello. *(Vincent nods.)* Nice Evening. *(Silence.)* God. *What a night.* Love it. *(Silence. Looking out.)*   Stars. Wow, would you believe. Stars, stars, stars. *(Pause.)*
VINCENT.   Orion's belt. *(Bradley doesn't follow his comment. Vincent points upwards.)* The constellation. Orion the Hunter. That line of stars there forms his belt. See?
BRADLEY.   Uh-huh. *(Pause. Sips his drink. Vincent points to another part of the night sky.)*
VINCENT.   And of course, the Big Dipper.
BRADLEY.   Of course.
VINCENT.   And, using the two stars that form the front of the lip of the dipper as your guide, it leads to the...
BRADLEY.   The North Star.
VINCENT.   Yes. Good. Very good. You will never be lost. *(Both quietly laugh.)*
BRADLEY.   Jeez, it's a bit stuffy in there. With all of them.

7

It's nice to be with someone I can feel comfortable around. *(Vincent doesn't understand.)* Well, I mean, like you and me. We're — I mean, we don't exactly look like... *(Nods towards the people inside.)*

VINCENT. Ahhh. *(Bradley laughs nervously, relieved that Vincent has understood.)* Actually, I had not noticed. I do not really notice, or quite frankly care, if someone is Caucasian of oriental or...

BRADLEY. *(Interrupts, correcting Asian. Vincent doesn't understand.)* It's Asian, not oriental. *(Vincent still doesn't follow. Bradley, embarrassed, tries to explain.)* Asian, oriental. Black, negro. Woman, girl. Gay, homosexual ... Asian, oriental.

VINCENT. Ahhh. *(Pause.)* Orientals are rugs? *(Bradley nods sheepishly.)* I see. *(Vincent studies him for a moment, then goes back to sipping his red wine.)* You don't look familiar.

BRADLEY. First time.

VINCENT. You haven't been to one of these parties before? *(Bradley shakes his head.)* Hah! You're in for a wonderful surprise. Everyone here is as obnoxious as hell.

BRADLEY. I noticed.

VINCENT. *(Laughs, extends his hand.)* Vincent Chang...

BRADLEY. *(Overlapping.)* Chang! *(Bradley grabs Vincent's hand and manipulates it through the classic "right-on" handshake. Vincent watches it unfold.)* You don't have to tell me. Everybody knows who you are. Especially in the community. Not that you're not famous — I mean, walking down the street they'd notice you — but in the community, whew! Forget it.

VINCENT. Ahhh. And you?

BRADLEY. What?

VINCENT. Your name.

BRADLEY. Oh. Bradley Yamashita. *(Pronounced "Yamasheeta" by him. Bradley shakes his hand again. Vincent repeats name to himself, trying to remember where he's heard it. He pronounces the name correctly.)* This is an amazing business. It really is. It's an amazing business. One moment I'm this snotty nose kid watching you on TV and the next thing you know I'm standing next to you and we're talking and stuff and you know... *(Silence. Sips drinks. Looks at stars.)* Mr. Chang? Mr.

8

Chang? I think it's important that all of us know each other. Asian American actors. I think the two of us meeting is very important. The young and the old. We can learn from each other. We can. I mean, the way things are, the way they're going, Jesus. If we don't stick together who the hell is going —

VINCENT. *(Interrupts, waving at someone.)* Ah, Theodora. Hello!

BRADLEY. Wow...

VINCENT. Theodora Ando. The *Asian-American* actress.

BRADLEY. God, she's gorgeous.

VINCENT. *(Coldly.)* Don't turn your back on her. *(Bradley doesn't follow. Vincent mimes sticking a knife in and twisting it.)*

BRADLEY. *(Staring after a disappearing Theodora.)* Oh... *(Silence. They sip and stare out into the darkness. Bradley begins to turn and smile at Vincent in hopes that Vincent will recognize his face. Vincent does not.)* New York. Jesus, what a town. Do you spend much time out there? *(Vincent shrugs.)* Yeah. I've been out in New York. That's where they know me most. Out in New York. I come from San Francisco. That's where I was born and raised. Trained — ACT. But I've been out in New York. I just came back from there. A film of mine opened. New York Film Festival. Guillaume Bouchet, the French critic loved it.

VINCENT. *(Impressed.)* Guillaume Bouchet.

BRADLEY. Uh-huh. Called it one of the 10 best films of the year.

VINCENT. It's your film? You ... directed it? *(Bradley shakes his head.)* Wrote it?

BRADLEY. No, no, I'm in it. I'm the main actor in it.

VINCENT. *(Mutters under his breath.)* An actor...

BRADLEY. It's a Matthew Iwasaki film.

VINCENT. I have heard of him, yes. He does those low-budget...

BRADLEY. *(Interrupts, correcting.)* Independent.

VINCENT. Ahhh. *Independent movies* about ...

BRADLEY. *(Interrupts, correcting again.)* Films. Independent films, they play in art houses.

VINCENT.   Ahhhh. *Independent films* that play in *art houses* about people like... *(Nods to Bradley and to himself.)*
BRADLEY.   Uh-huh
VINCENT.   I see. Hmmm.
BRADLEY.   I'm in it. I star in it. Eugene Bickle...
VINCENT.   *(Interrupts.)* Who?
BRADLEY.   Eugene Bickle, the film critic on TV. You know, everybody knows about him. He used to be on PBS and now he's on the networks with that other fat guy. He said I was one of the most "watchable" stars he's seen this year.
VINCENT.   Really?
BRADLEY.   He said he wouldn't mind watching me no matter what I was doing.
VINCENT.   *Really?*
BRADLEY.   Well, that's not exactly — I'm sort of paraphrasing, but that's what he meant. Not that he'd wanna watch me doing anything — you know, walking down the street. But on the screen. In another movie.
VINCENT.   Film.
BRADLEY.   What?
VINCENT.   You said "another movie."
BRADLEY.   Film.
VINCENT.   Ahh.
BRADLEY.   My agent at William Morris wanted me to come to L.A. I have an audition on Monday. One of the big theatres.
VINCENT.   *(Impressed, but hiding it.)* William Morris?
BRADLEY.   *(Notices that Vincent is impressed.)* Uh-huh. *(Pause.)* Who handles you?
VINCENT.   Snow Kwong-Johnson.
BRADLEY.   Oh. *(Pause.)* I hear they handle mainly...
VINCENT.   *(Interrupts.)* She.
BRADLEY.   Oh, yes. *She* handles mainly... *(Motions to Vincent and himself.)*
VINCENT.   Yes. Mainly... *(Motions to Bradley and to himself.)*
BRADLEY.   Ahhh, I see. Well. *(Silence.)*
VINCENT.   It's a bit warm tonight.

10

BRADLEY.   I feel fine, just fine. *(Vincent takes a cigarette out and is about to smoke. Bradley begins to steal glances at Vincent's face. Vincent remembers to offer one to Bradley.)* I don't smoke. *(The mood is ruined for Vincent. He puts the cigarette away. About to take a sip of his red wine. Bradley notices Vincent's drink.)* Tanins. Bad for the complexion. *(Holds up his drink.)* Club soda.

VINCENT.   I imagine you exercise, too?

BRADLEY.   I swim three times a week. Do you work out?

VINCENT.   Yes. Watch. *(Lifts drink to his lips and gulps it down. Pause. Vincent notices Bradley looking at his face. Bradley realizes he's been caught, feigns ignorance, and looks away. Vincent touches his face to see if he has a piece of food on his cheek, or something worse on his nose. Vincent's not sure of Bradley's intent. Perhaps he was admiring his good looks. Vincent's not sure.)* Bradley? Was there something? You were ... looking at me? *(Vincent motions gracefully towards his face. Pause. Bradley decides to explain.)*

BRADLEY.   This is kind of personal, I know. I don't know if I should ask you. *(Pause.)* Ok, is that your real nose?

VINCENT.   What?

BRADLEY.   I mean, your original one — you know, the one you were born with?

VINCENT.   *(Smile fading.)* What?

BRADLEY.   Someone once told me — and if it's not true just say so — someone once told me you hold the record for "noses." *(Barely able to contain his giggling.)* You've had all these different noses. Sinatra, Montgomery Clift, Troy Donahue — whatever was *in* at the time. Sort of like the "7 Noses of Dr. Lao..." *(Notices Vincent is not laughing.)* That's what they said. I just thought maybe I would ask you about...

VINCENT.   *(Interrupts.)* Who told you this?

BRADLEY.   No one.

VINCENT.   You said someone told you.

BRADLEY.   Yes, but...

VINCENT.   *(Interrupts.)* Someone is usually a person. And if this person *told you* it means he probably has lips. Who is this person with *big, fat, moving* lips.

BRADLEY.   I don't know, just someone. I forget — I'm not good at remembering lips.

VINCENT. No. *(Bradley doesn't follow.)* No, it is *not* true. This is my natural nose. As God is my witness. *(Silence. Vincent sipping drink. Turns to look at Bradley. Repeating the name to himself.)* Yamashita ... Ya-ma-shita ... You worked with Chloe Fong in New York? *(Bradley nods.)* Ahhh.

BRADLEY. What? *(Vincent ignores Bradley's query and goes back to staring out at the night sky. Occasionally, glances at Bradley knowingly.)* What? *(Pause.)*

VINCENT. Now this is kind of personal. And tell me if I am wrong. I heard you almost got fired in New York.

BRADLEY. Who said that — what?

VINCENT. You are the fellow who was out in that play in New York, correct? With Chloe?

BRADLEY. Yeah, so?

VINCENT. I heard — and tell me if I am wrong, rumors are such vicious things — I heard they were not too happy with you, your work.

BRADLEY. What do you mean, "not happy with me?"

VINCENT. Now, this is probably just a rumor — I do not know — But, that is what I...

BRADLEY. *(Interrupts.)* That's not true. That's not true at all. I was a little nervous, so was everybody. And I never, "almost got fired." Did Chloe say that?

VINCENT. No, no, no.

BRADLEY. Cause I was OK. Once I got comfortable I was good. You ask Chloe. The director came up afterwards and congratulated me he liked my work so much. White director.

VINCENT. Ah, rumors.

BRADLEY. *(Mutters under his breath.)* Bull shit... *(Silence. Vincent takes a cigarette out, lights it and takes a deep, satisfying drag.)*

VINCENT. Ahhh. I needed that. *(Pause.)*

BRADLEY. Who said I almost got fired? Was it Chloe? She wouldn't say something like that. I know her. *(Beat.)* Was it her?

VINCENT. It is just a rumor. Take it easy. Just a rumor. Remember this? *(Taps his nose.)* Dr. Lao? It comes with the terrain. You must learn to live with it. It happens to

12

everyone. Sooner or later. *Everyone.* You are walking along, minding your own business, your head filled with poems and paintings — when what do you see coming your way? Some ugly "rumor," dressed in your clothes, staggering down the street impersonating you. And it is not you but no one seems to care. They want this impersonator — who is drinking from a brown paper bag, whose pant zipper is down to here and flapping in the wind — to be you. Why? They like it. It gives them glee. They like the lie. And the more incensed you become, the more real it seems to grow. Like some monster in a nightmare. If you ignore it, you rob it of its strength. It will soon disappear. *(Beat.)* You will live. We all go to bed thinking, "The pain is so great, I will not last through the night." *(Beat.)* We wake up. Alive. C'est dommage. *(Pause.)* Have you seen my latest film? It has been out for several months.

BRADLEY.   Was this the Ninja assassin one?

VINCENT.   No, that was 3 years ago. This one deals with life after the atomic holocaust and dramatizes how post-nuclear man must deal with what has become, basically, a very very hostile environ...

BRADLEY.   *(Interrupts.)*   Oh, the one with the mutant monsters — they moved all jerky, Ray Harryhausen stuff — and the hairy guys eating raw meat? You were in that film? I saw that film.

VINCENT.   I got billing. I got...

BRADLEY.   You were in it?

VINCENT.   ...the box.

BRADLEY.   I'm sure I saw that film. *(Looking at Vincent's face.)*

VINCENT.   I came in after everyone signed so my name is in the square box. My name...

BRADLEY.   Nah, you weren't in it. I saw that film.

VINCENT.   ...is in all the ads. There is a big marquee as you drive down Sunset Boulevard with my name in that box.

BRADLEY.   *(Staring at Vincent's face, it's coming to him.)*   Oh, oh ... You were the husband of the woman who was eaten by the giant salamander? *(Bradley is having a hard time suppressing his laughter.)*

VINCENT. *(Shrugging.)* It was a little hard to tell, I know. The make-up was a little heavy. But it was important to create characters that in some way reflected the effects...

BRADLEY. *(Overlapping, can no longer contain himself and bursts out laughing.)* Make-up a little heavy? Jesus Christ, you had so much hair on your face you looked like a fucking chimpanzee! *(Bradley stops laughing as he notices Vincent's pained expression. Awkward silence. Vincent smokes his cigarette. Bradley sips on his soda. Bradley occasionally steals a glance at Vincent. Vincent watches the North Star. Dim to darkness.)*

End of Scene

Scene Two

"WIN ONE FOR THE NIPPER"

Audition waiting room at a theater. Vincent seated, reading a magazine. Bradley enters, carrying script.

BRADLEY. *(Calls back.)* Yeah, thanks, ten minutes. *(Bradley sees Vincent, cautiously seats himself. Vincent pretends not to notice Bradley and turns away from him, still buried in his magazine. They sit in silence. Breaking the ice.)* Mr. Chang, I'm sorry. I really didn't mean to laugh...

VINCENT. *(Interrupts.)* Excuse me young man, but do I know you?

BRADLEY. Well, yes ... we met at that party over the weekend in the Hollywood Hills...

VINCENT. *(Interrupts.)* What did you say your name was?

BRADLEY. Bradley. Bradley Yamashita.

VINCENT. And we met at that party?

BRADLEY. Yeah. On the balcony. *(Vincent stares intently at Bradley who is becoming uncomfortable.)*

VINCENT. You look familiar. You must forgive me. I go to so many parties. Did I make a fool of myself? I do that sometimes. I drink too much and do not remember a

14

thing. That makes me an angel. You see, angels have no memories. *(Vincent smiles and goes back to reading.)*
BRADLEY. Look, whether you want to remember or not, that's your business. But I'm sorry, Mr. Chang. I sincerely apologize. I can't do more than that. I shouldn't have laughed at you. *(Silence.)*
VINCENT. You say your name is Bradley? Bradley Yamashita? *(Bradley nods.)* Which part in the play are you reading for?
BRADLEY. The son.
VINCENT. They want me for the part of the father. I am meeting the director. We could end up father and son. It might prove to be interesting.
BRADLEY. Yeah.
VINCENT. Then again, it might not. *(Silence. Awkward moment. Vincent studies Bradley.)* Maybe they will cast Theodora Ando. As your sister. Make it a *murder* mystery. *(Vincent mimes stabbing with a knife and twisting the blade. Bradley recalls Vincent's earlier reference to Theodora at the party and laughs. Vincent laughs, also. Pause.)*
BRADLEY. You know, Mr. Chang, when I was growing up you were sort of my hero. No, really, you were. I mean, I'd be watching TV and suddenly you'd appear in some old film or an old Bonanza or something. And at first something would always jerk inside. Whoo, what's this? This is weird, like watching my own family on TV. It's like the first time I made it with an Asian girl — up to then only white girls. They seemed more outgoing — I don't know — more normal. With this Asian girl it was like doing it with my sister. It was weird. Everything about her was familiar. Her face, her skin, the sound of her voice, the way she smelled. It was like having sex with someone in my own family. That's how it was when you'd come on the TV. You were kind of an idol. *(Pause.)*
VINCENT. You know who I wanted to be like? You know who my hero was? Fred Astaire. *(Noticing Bradley's look.)* Yes, Fred Astaire.
BRADLEY. You danced?
VINCENT. *(Nods.)* Un-huh.

BRADLEY.   I didn't know that.

VINCENT.   Yes, well... *(Awkward pause. Both want to pursue conversation but unsure how to. Vincent starts to go back to script.)*

BRADLEY.   What kind of dancing did you do? I mean, Fred Astaire kind of dancing or Gene Kelly-like, or, or, like the Nicholas Brothers — flying off those risers, landing doing the splits — ouch!

VINCENT.   *(Laughs.)* You know who the Nicholas Brothers are?

BRADLEY.   Yeah, sure, of course. And Fred Astaire — Jesus, so smooth. I loved him in *Silk Stockings*. And Cyd Charisse was great.

VINCENT.   No, no, *Ginger Rogers, Top Hat*. The two of them together, Ahhh. *(Silence.)*

BRADLEY.   Would you show me something? *(Vincent doesn't follow.)* Some dance moves.

VINCENT.   Now? Right here?

BRADLEY.   Yeah, come on, just a little.

VINCENT.   No, no, I haven't danced in years.

BRADLEY.   Come on, Vincent. I'd love to see you...

VINCENT.   *(Overlapping.)*   No, no, I can't.

BRADLEY.   ...dance. No one's around. Come on, Vincent, I'd love to see it.

VINCENT.   Well. Alright. *(He gets up.)* A little soft-shoe routine... *(Vincent does a small sampling of some dance moves ending with a small flourish.)*

BRADLEY.   *(Applauds.)* Great! That was great!

VINCENT.   Back then you did everything. Tell jokes, juggle, sing — The Kanazawa Trio, great jugglers. Oh, and Jade Wing, a wonderful, wonderful, dancer. The Wongettes — like the Andrews Sisters. On and on, all great performers. We all worked the Chop Suey Circuit.

BRADLEY.   Chop Suey Circuit?

VINCENT.   In San Francisco you had of course, Forbidden City, Kubla Kan, New York's China Doll — some of the greatest oriental acts ever to go down. That's my theater background. *(Vincent tries to catch his breath.)* See, there was this one routine that Jade — Jade Wing, she was my partner — and I did that was special. We had developed it ourselves and at the end we did this spectacular move where I pull her up on my shoulders, she falls back, and as she's falling I reach under, grab her hands and pull her through my legs thrusting her into the air ... And I catch her! Tadah! We were rather famous for it. This one night we performed it — we were in town here, I forget the name of the club — and as the audience began to clap, these two people at one of the front tables stood up, applauding enthusiastically. Everyone followed. It was an amazing feeling to have the whole house on their feet. And then we saw the two people leading the standing ovation. We couldn't believe our eyes — Anna Mae Wong, the "Chinese Flapper" herself, and Sessue Hayakawa. The two most famous oriental stars of the day. They invited us to their table, Hayakawa with his fancy French cigarettes and his thick accent. It was a good thing that I spoke Japanese.

BRADLEY.   You speak Japanese?

VINCENT.   A little, I speak a little. But Anna Mae Wong spoke impeccable English. In fact, she had an English accent, can you believe that? "Vincent, you danced like you were floating on air." We nearly died then and there. Jade and I sitting at the same table with Anna Mae and Sessue.

BRADLEY.   God, wasn't Anna Mae gorgeous.

VINCENT.   Yes. But not as pretty as Jade Wing. I think Anna Mae Wong was a little jealous of all the attention Sessue was paying to Jade. God, Jade was beautiful. She was 23 when I met her. I was just 19. She was a burlesque dancer at the Forbidden City.

BRADLEY.   What? Did you two have a thing going on or something?

VINCENT.   For a while. But things happen. You are on the road continuously. She wanted one thing, I wanted another. I was pretty wild in those days. There were things about me she just could not accept. That was a long, long time ago.

BRADLEY.   What happened to her?

VINCENT.   I do not know. I heard she ended up marrying someone up in San Francisco who owned a bar in Chinatown. I forget the name of the bar — "Gumbo's" or some such name. I always meant to go and see her.

BRADLEY. I've been there a couple of times. There's...

VINCENT. *(Overlapping.)* I think she may have passed away. She was...

BRADLEY. ...this old woman who runs it, a grouchy old bitch...

VINCENT. ...so beautiful... *(Awkward pause. Vincent had heard Bradley speak of the old woman.)* Remember this? *(Re-enacting a scene from his most famous role.)* "A sleep that will take an eternity to wash away the weariness that I now feel."

BRADLEY. I know that, I know that ... *Tears of Winter,* opposite Peter O'Toole. You were nominated for best supporting actor! It's out on video, I have it. I know it by heart. *(Vincent feels good. Decides to launch into the whole scene. Saki is mortally wounded.)*

VINCENT. *(As Saki.)* Death is a funny thing Master Abrams. You spend your entire life running from its toothless grin. Yet, when you are face to face with it, death is friendly. It smiles and beckons to you like some long lost lover. And you find yourself wanting, more than anything in the world, to rest, to sleep in her open inviting arms. A sleep that will take an eternity to wash away the weariness that I now feel. *(Vincent stumbles towards Bradley.)*

BRADLEY. Vincent? *(Vincent collapses into Bradley's unexpecting arms. They tumble to the ground. Vincent, cradled in Bradley's arms, looks up at him.)* You surprised me.

VINCENT. Don't speak.

BRADLEY. What?

VINCENT. Don't speak. That's your line, Peter O'Toole's line. *Don't speak.*

BRADLEY. Oh-oh. Don't speak, Saki. You must save your strength. We did the best we could. All is lost my little "nipper." The dream is dead. *(Saki is fading fast. Starts to close eyes. Then suddenly.)*

VINCENT. *No!* A dream does not die with one man's death, Master. Think of all the women, children, and babies who will suffer if we are defeated. You must smash the enemy! You must win! *(Pause. Coughs up blood. Continues with heroic efforts.)* Then I can sleep the final sleep with only one dream, the most important dream to keep me company on my journey through hell. *(Vincent nudges Bradley to feed him his line.)*

BRADLEY.   What dream is that Saki?

VINCENT.   The dream of *victory! (Saki gasps for life.)* Master...

BRADLEY.   Yes?

VINCENT.   Win one for the ... Nipper. *(Saki dies in his master's arms.)*

BRADLEY.   Saki? Saki? *(He bows his grief-stricken head in Saki's breast. Then, recovering.)* Oh, you were great in that film. Great.

VINCENT.   You weren't so bad yourself. *(Bradley helps Vincent to his feet.)* I'm ready for the director now.

BRADLEY.   Can I run my audition piece for you? This is the first Asian American play I ever saw. Characters up there talking to me, something inside of me, not some white guy. I'd never experienced anything...

VINCENT.   *(Interrupts.)* Just do it, do it. Don't explain it away. *(Bradley stands in silence. Closes eyes. Shrugs, fidgets, clears throat. Opens eyes, finally, and begins.)*

BRADLEY.   It was night. It was one of those typical summer nights in the Valley. The hot dry heat of the day was gone. Just the night air filled with swarming mosquitoes, the sound of those irrigation pumps sloshing away. And that peculiar smell that comes from those empty fruit crates stacked in the sheds with their bits and pieces of mashed apricots still clinging to the sides and bottom. They've been sitting in the moist heat of the packing sheds all day long. And by evening they fill the night air with that unmistakable pungent odor of sour and sweet that only a summer night, a summer night in the San Joaquin Valley can give you. And that night, as with every night, I was lost. And that night, as with every night of my life, I was looking for somewhere, someplace that belonged to me. I took my Dad's car 'cause I just had to go for a drive. "Where you going son? We got more work to do in the sheds separating out the

19

fruit." "Sorry, Dad ..." I'd drive out to the Yonemoto's and pick up my girl, Bess. Her mother'd say, "Drive carefully and take good care of my daughter — She's Pa and me's only girl." "Sure, Mrs. Yonemoto..." And I'd drive. Long into the night. Windows down, my girl Bess beside me, the radio blasting away ... But it continued to escape me — this thing, place, that belonged to me ... And then the DJ came on the radio, "Here's a new record by a hot new artist, 'Carol' by Neil Sedaka!" Neil who? Sedaka? Did you say, "Sedaka." *(Pronunciation gradually becomes Japanese.)* Sedaka. Sedaka. Sedaka. *Sedaakaa.* As in my father's cousin's brother-in-law's name, Hiroshi Sedaka? What's that you say — the first Japanese American rock 'n roll star! Neil Sedaka. That name. I couldn't believe it. Suddenly everything was alright. I was there. Driving in my car, windows down, girl beside me — with a goddamned Buddhahead singing on the radio ... Neil Sedaakaa! I knew. I just knew for once, where ever I drove to that night, the road belonged to me. *(Silence.)*

VINCENT.   Bradley? Neil Sedaka is not Japanese.

BRADLEY.   Yes, I know.

VINCENT.   I have met him before. He's Jewish, or was it Lebanese. Very nice fellow. But definitely not Japanese.

BRADLEY.   Yes, yes, I know. It's by Robinson Kan, the sansei playwright. It shows the need we have for legitimate heroes. And how when you don't have any, just how far you'll go to make them up.

VINCENT.   Yes, yes. Well ... *(Awkward pause.)* Say, do you sing?

BRADLEY.   "Scoshi", a little.

VINCENT.   Do you know the musical I was in, *Tea Cakes and Moon Songs?* Sure you do. Let's do Charlie Chop Suey's love song to Mei Ling. I'll play Charlie the Waiter and you play Mei Ling.

BRADLEY.   Mei Ling?

VINCENT.   *(Dragging Bradley about.)* Your part is easy. All you have to do is stand there and sing, "So Sorry, Charlie." You hit the gong. *(Standing side by side. Vincent provides classic sing-songey intro.)* Da Da Da Da - Dah Dah Dah Dah Dah Da Da Da Dah Dah DAH! *(Vincent looks expectantly at Bradley who doesn't have a clue and is feeling ridiculous.)* You hit the gong. You hit the gong. *(Vincent demonstrates, then quickly hums intro and starts the song. Bradley feels awkward but is swept along by the enthusiasm of Vincent. Vincent singing.)*

Tea cakes and moon songs
June bugs and love gongs
I feel like dancing with you.
Roast duck and dao fu
Lop chong and char siu
Strolling down Grant Avenue
Chorus: Da Da Da Da — Dah Dah Dah Dah Dah
So Solly Cholly.

(As they dance around, Bradley coquettishly hiding behind a fan, Vincent urges him to make his voice more female sounding.) Higher, make your voice higher! Da Da Da Da — Dah Dah Dah Dah Dah.

BRADLEY.   *(Struggling to go higher.)* So Solly Cholly!

VINCENT.   Higher! Higher!

BRADLEY.   *(Falsetto.)* So Solly Cholly! *(They are whirling around the stage. Vincent singing and tap dancing with Bradley in tow singing in a high pitched falsetto. Both are getting more and more involved, acting out more and more outrageous stereotypes. Bradley slowly starts to realize what he's doing.)* Wait, wait, wait, what is this — WAIT! What am I doing? What is this shit? (Then accusingly to Vincent who has gradually stopped.) You're acting like a Chinese Steppin Fetchit. That's what you're acting like. Jesus, fucking Christ, Vincent. A *Chinese Steppin Fetchit.* (Bradley exits. Vincent glares in the direction of his exit.)

End of Scene

INTERLUDE 2

Vincent lit in pool of light accepting an award.

VINCENT. This is a great honor. A great honor, indeed. To be recognized by my fellow Asian American actors in the industry. I have been criticized. Yes, I am aware of that. But I am an actor. Not a writer. I can only speak the words that are written for me. I am an actor. Not a politician. I cannot change the world. I can only bring life, through truth and craft, to my characterizations. I have never turned down a role. Good or bad, the responsibility of an actor is to do that role well. That is all an actor should or has to be concerned about. Acting. Whatever is asked of you, do it. Yes. But do it with dignity. I am an actor. *(Vincent dims to darkness. Flash! Bradley lit in pool of light. Holding a camera that has just flashed. Wearing stereotypic glasses. He is at an audition for a commercial.)*

BRADLEY. What? Take the picture, then put my hand like this — in front of my mouth and *giggle*? Yeah, but Japanese men don't giggle. How about if I shoot the picture and like this ... Just laugh. *(Listens.)* I'm sorry but I can't do that. Look, it's not truthful to the character. Japanese men don't giggle. What? *(Listens. Turns to leave.)* Yeah, well the same to you Mr. Ass-hole director. *(Dim to darkness on Bradley. We hear a glitzy, Las Vegas version of Tea Cakes and Moon Songs. Vincent lit in a pool of light. Wearing a big cowboy hat. He is the master of ceremonies at a huge Tupperware convention in Houston. Holding mike.)*

VINCENT. Howdy! Howdy! It is good to be here in Houston, Texas. In case you don't know me, I'm Vincent Chang. *(Applause.)* Thank you, thank you. And if you do not know who I am, shame on you! And, go out and buy a copy of *Tears of Winter.* It is out on video now I understand. Hey, you know what they call Chinese blindfolds? *Dental Floss!*

(Laughter.) And I would especially like to thank Tupperware for inviting me to be your master-of-ceremonies at your annual national — no, I take that back — your *international* convention. *(Applause, and more applause.)* Yeah! Yeah! What's the word? *(Holds mike out to audience.)* TUPPERWARE! Yeah! What's the word? *(Vincent holds mike out to the audience. Blackout on Vincent. Bradley lit talking to his Asian actor friends.)*

BRADLEY.   I can't believe this business with the Asian American awards. I mean it's a joke — there aren't enough decent roles for us in a year. What? An award for the best Asian American actor in the role of Vietnamese killer. *(Mimicking sarcastically.)* And now in the category of "Best Actress with 5 lines or Less..." That's all we get. Who're we kidding. This business. This goddamned fucking business. And I can't believe they gave that award to Vincent Chang. *Vincent Chang.* His speech — "I never turned down a role." Shi-it! *(Dim to darkness.)*

End of Interlude

Scene Three

"THEY EDITED IT OUT"

After an acting class. Vincent is upset. Bradley packing his duffle bag.

VINCENT.   You do not know a thing about the industry. Not a damn thing. Who the hell...

BRADLEY.   *(Interrupts, calling to someone across the room.)* Yeah, Alice — I'll get my lines down for our scene, sorry.

VINCENT.   *(Attempts to lower his voice so as not to be heard.)* Who the hell are you to talk to me that way. Been in the business a few...

BRADLEY.   *(Interrupts.)* Look, if I offended you last time by something I said I'm sorry. I like your work, Mr. Chang. You know that. I like your...

VINCENT. *(Interrupts.)* A "Chinese Steppin Fetchit" — that is what you called me. A "Chinese Steppin Fetchit." Remember?

BRADLEY. I'm an angel, OK, I'm an angel. *No memory.*

VINCENT. And you do not belong in this class.

BRADLEY. My agent at William Morris arranged for me to join this class.

VINCENT. This is for *advanced* actors.

BRADLEY. I've been acting in the theatre for 7 years, Mr. Chang.

VINCENT. 7 years? 7 years? 7 years is a wink of an eye. An itch on the ass. A fart in my sleep my fine, feathered friend.

BRADLEY. I've been acting at the Theatre Project of Asian America in San Francisco for 7 years — acting, directing, writing...

VINCENT. Poppycock, Cockypoop, bullshit. Theatre Project of Asian America — "Amateur Hour."

BRADLEY. "Amateur hour?" Asian American theaters are where we do the real work, Mr. Chang.

VINCENT. The business, Bradley, I am talking about the business, the industry. That Matthew Iwasaki movie was a fluke, an accident...

BRADLEY. *(Interrupts.)* Film, Mr. Chang.

VINCENT. *Movie!* And stop calling me Mr. Chang. It's Shigeo Nakada. "Asian American consciousness." Hah. You can't even tell the difference between a Chinaman and a Jap. I'm Japanese, didn't you know that? I changed my name after the war. Hell, I wanted to work...

BRADLEY. *(Mutters.)* You are so jive, Mr. Chang...

VINCENT. You think you're better than I, don't you? Somehow special, above it all. The new generation. With all your fancy politics about this Asian American new-way-of-thinking and 7 long years of paying your dues at Asian Project Theater or whatever it is. You don't know shit my friend. You don't know the meaning of paying your dues in this business.

BRADLEY. The business. You keep talking about the business. The industry. Hollywood. What's Hollywood? Cutting up your face to look more white? So my nose is a little flat. Fine! Flat is beautiful. So I don't have a double-fold in my eyelid. Great! No one in my entire racial family has had it in the last 10,000 years. My old girlfriend used to put scotch tape on her eyelids to get the double fold so she could look more "cau-ca-sian." My new girlfriend — she doesn't mess around, she got surgery. Where does it begin? Vincent? All that self hate, *where does it begin?* You and your Charley Chop Suey roles...

VINCENT. You want to know the truth? I'm glad I did it. Yes, you heard me right. I'm glad I did it and I'm not ashamed, I wanted to do it. And no one is ever going to get an apology out of me. And in some small way it is a victory. Yes, a victory. At least an oriental was on screen acting, being seen. We existed.

BRADLEY. But that's not existing — wearing some god-damn monkey suit and kissing up to some white man, that's not existing.

VINCENT. That's all there was, Bradley. That's all there was! But you don't think I wouldn't have wanted to play a better role than that bucktoothed, groveling waiter? I would have killed for a better role where I could have played an honest-to-god human being with real emotions. I would have killed for it. You seem to assume "Asian Americans" always existed. That there were always roles for you. You didn't exist back then buster. Back then there was no Asian American consciousness, no Asian American actor, and no Asian American theaters. Just a handful of "orientals" who for some god forsaken reason wanted to perform. *Act.* And we did. At church bazaars, community talent night, and on the Chop Suey Circuit playing Chinatowns and Little Tokyos around the country as hoofers, jugglers, acrobats, strippers — anything we could for anyone who would watch. You, you with that holier than thou look, trying to make me feel ashamed. You wouldn't be here if it weren't for all the crap we had put up with. We built something. We built the mountain, as small as it may be, that you stand on so proudly looking down at me. Sure, it's a mountain of Charley Chop Suey's and slipper-toting geishas. But it is also filled with forgotten moments of extraordinary wonder, artistic achievement. A singer, Larry Ching, he could croon like Frank Sinatra and better looking, too. Ever heard of him? Toy Yet Mar — boy, she could belt it out with the best of them. "The Chinese Sophie Tucker." No one's ever heard of her. And Dorothy Takahashi, she could dance the high heels off of anyone, Ginger Rodgers included. And, who in the hell has ever heard of Fred Astaire and Dorothy Takahashi? Dead dreams, my friend. Dead dreams, broken backs and long forgotten beauty. I swear sometimes when I'm taking my curtain call I can see this shadowy figure out of the corner of my eye taking the most glorious, dignified bow. Who remembers? *Who* appreciates?

BRADLEY.   See, you think every time you do one of those demeaning roles, the only thing lost is *your* dignity. That the only person who has to pay is you. Don't you see that every time you do that millions of people in movie theaters will see it. Believe it. Every time you do any old stereotypic role just to pay the bills, someone has to pay for it — and it ain't you. *No.* It's some Asian kid innocently walking home. "Hey, it's a Chinaman gook!" "Rambo, Rambo, Rambo!" You older actors. You ask to be understood, forgiven, but you refuse to change. You have no sense of social responsibility. Only me...

VINCENT.   *(Overlapping.)*   No...

BRADLEY.   ... me, me. Shame on you. I'd never play a role like that stupid waiter in that musical. And...

VINCENT.   You don't know...

BRADLEY.   ...I'd never let them put so much make-up on my face that I look like some goddamn chimpanzee on the screen.

VINCENT.   *(Overlapping.)*   You don't know...

BRADLEY.   I don't care if they paid me a million dollars, what good is it to lose your dignity. I'm not going to prostitute my soul just to...

VINCENT.   *(Overlapping.)*   There's *that* word. I was wondering when we'd get around to that word. I hate that word! I HATE THAT WORD!

BRADLEY.   ... see myself on screen if I have to go grunting around like some slant-eyed animal. You probably wouldn't know a good role if it grabbed you by the balls!

VINCENT.   I have played many good roles.

BRADLEY.   Sure, waiters, Viet Cong killers, chimpanzees, drug dealers, hookers —

VINCENT.   *(Interrupts.)*   I was the first to be nominated for an Academy Award.

BRADLEY.   Oh, it's pull-out-the-old-credits time. But what about some of the TV stuff you've been doing lately. Jesus, TV! At least in the movies we're still dangerous. But TV? They fucking cut off our balls and made us all house boys on the evening soaps. *(Calls out.)* "Get your very own neutered, oriental houseboy!"

VINCENT.   I got the woman once. *(Bradley doesn't understand.)* In the movie. I got the woman.

BRADLEY.   Sure.

VINCENT.   And she was *white.*

BRADLEY.   You're so full of it.

VINCENT.   And I kissed her!

BRADLEY.   What, a peck on the cheek?

VINCENT.   ON THE LIPS! ON THE LIPS! *I GOT THE WOMAN.*

BRADLEY.   Nah.

VINCENT.   Yes.

BRADLEY.   Nah?

VINCENT.   *YES.*

BRADLEY.   *(Pondering.)* When was this? In the 30's. Before the war?

VINCENT.   *(Overlapping.)* No.

BRADLEY.   Because that happened back then. After the war forget it. Mr. Moto even disappeared and he was played by Peter Lorre.

VINCENT.   No, no. This was the 50's.

BRADLEY.   Come on, you're kidding.

27

VINCENT. 1959. A cop movie. *(Correcting himself.)* Film. *The Scarlet Kimono.* Directed by Sam Fuller. Set in L.A. 2 police detectives, one Japanese American and one Caucasian. And a beautiful blond, they both love.

BRADLEY. Yeah ... I remember. And there's this violent kendo fight between you two guys because you both want the woman. *(Realizing.)* And you get the woman.

VINCENT. See, I told you so. *(Pause. Bradley seated himself.)*

BRADLEY. Except when I saw it you didn't kiss her. I mean I would have remembered something like that. An Asian man and a white woman. You didn't kiss her.

VINCENT. TV?

BRADLEY. Late Night. *(Bradley nods. Vincent making the realization.)*

VINCENT. They edited it out. *(Silence. Vincent is upset. Bradley watches him. Dim to darkness.)*

End of Scene

INTERLUDE 3

Darkness. Bradley lit in pool of light. Silently practicing "tai-chi," with dark glasses on. His movements are graceful, fluid. Stops. Poised in silence like a statue. Suddenly breaks into savage kung-fu kicks with the accompanying Bruce Lee screams. Stops. Silence. Bradley shakes himself as if trying to release pent-up tension. Quietly begins the graceful "tai-chi" movement. Bradley dims to darkness and Vincent lit in pool of light.

VINCENT. *(On the phone to Kenneth.)* I can not. You know why. Someone might see us together. *(Listens.)* You do not know. People talk. Especially in this oriental community and then what happens to my career. I am a leading man. *(Kenneth hangs up on him.)* I am a leading man. *(Dim to darkness.)*

End of Interlude

Scene Four

"THE LOOK IN THEIR EYES"

After acting class, Vincent and Bradley in a crowded, noisy bar having a drink. They play a raucous verbal game.

BRADLEY.   Mr. Chang, it's a...
VINCENT.   *(Interrupts, calls to a waitress.)* Excuse me! Tanquery martini, straight up with a twist. Dry.
BRADLEY.   *(Pretending to be a casting agent making an offer.)* Mr. Chang, it's a 2 day contract.
VINCENT.   *(No accent, straight, not much effort.)* Yankee dog, you die.
BRADLEY.   *(Trying to suppress his laughter.)* Mr. Chang, it's a "1 week" contract. And don't forget the residuals when this goes into syndication.
VINCENT.   *(Big "oriental" accent. Barely able to contain his laughter.)* Yankee dawg, you die!
BRADLEY.   Mr. Chang, it's a "3 month shoot" on location in the "Caribbean Islands." Vincent, we're talking a cool 6 figures here. You can get your condo in Malibu, your silver mercedes, you'll...
VINCENT.   *(Overlapping. An outrageous caricature, all the while barely containing his laughter.)* YANKEE DAWG YOU DIE! YANKEE DAWG YOU DIE! YANKEE DAWG YOU DIE!
BRADLEY.   ...BE LYING ON SOME BEACH IN ST. TROPEZ, GETTING A TAN, HAVING A GOOD OLE TIME!...
VINCENT.   My drink... *(Both calm down.)*
BRADLEY.   I talked my agent into getting me an audition. It's that new lawyer series. He was very reluctant, the role wasn't written for an Asian. I said, "Jason, just get me in there." I showed up for the audition. I said, "I can do it, I can do it." They said, "No, the character's name is Jones." I said, "I can play a character named Jones." They said, "No." "I was adopted." "No." "I married a women and gave up my name." "No." Hell, if some white guy can play Chan, some

29

yellow guy can play Jones. *(Pause. Sipping drinks.)*

VINCENT.   Do you remember that film, *Bad Day At Black Rock?*

BRADLEY.   *(Remembering.)*   Yeah, yeah...

VINCENT.   That role, that role that Spencer Tracy plays?

BRADLEY.   Yeah, but it's about some Nisei 442 vet, right?

VINCENT.   That's who the story revolves around but he does not appear. He's dead. Got killed saving Tracy's life in Italy. After the war Tracy goes to the dead soldier's home town to return a war medal to his Issei parents. Only they don't appear either. Their farm is burned down, they are missing, and therein lies the tale. I should have played that role.

BRADLEY.   Whose role? Spencer Tracy's?

VINCENT.   It's about a Nisei.

BRADLEY.   Yeah, but none appear.

VINCENT.   But he could have been a Nisei, Tracy's character. And I have always felt I should have played it.

BRADLEY.   Me. Robert De Niro, Taxi Driver. "You talking to me? You talking to me?"

VINCENT.   *Harvey.*

BRADLEY.   Keitel?

VINCENT.   No, no. The film with Jimmy Stewart.

BRADLEY.   With the rabbit? The big fucking rabbit nobody can see?

VINCENT.   God, Stewart's role is wonderful. Everyone thinks he is mad, but he is not. He is not. Original innocence.

BRADLEY.   Mickey Rourke in Pope of Greenwich Village. "Hit me again — see if I change."

VINCENT.   James Dean, East of Eden, Salinas, a farm boy just like me. *(As Vincent enacts a scene from the movie, Bradley appears quiet and momentarily lost in thought.)*

BRADLEY.   *(Interrupts.)*   Forget what I said about Mickey Rourke. He's an ass-hole — he did that *Year of the Dragon.* I hated that film.

VINCENT.   Not that film again. It is ... just a "movie." *(Calls after waitress who seems to be ignoring him.)* My drink! *(They sip in silence. Bradley reaches into his bag and pulls out a script.)*

BRADLEY.   Vincent? Want to work on something together?

VINCENT.   We already are taking the same class...

BRADLEY.   *(Interrupts.)* No, no, over at the Asian American Theater. The one here in town.

VINCENT.   No, no, all those orientals huddling together, scared of the outside world — it is stifling to an actor's need for freedom.

BRADLEY.   It's a workshop production, a new play by Robinson Kan — a sci-fi, political drama about...

VINCENT.   *(Interrupts.)* You should be out there doing the classics, Bradley. It is limiting, seeing yourself just as an Asian. And you must never limit yourself. Never. *(Bradley reaches into his bag and pulls out a small Godzilla toy.)*

BRADLEY.   It's got Godzilla in it.

VINCENT.   Godzilla? *(Moving it playfully.)* Godzilla. Aahk. *(Calling to waitress.)* My drink, *please.*

BRADLEY.   You can do and say whatever you want there.

VINCENT.   An actor must be free. You must understand that. *Free.*

BRADLEY.   And they will never edit it out. *(Awkward silence. Sipping.)* I was in a theater in Westwood. I was there with a bunch of Asian friends. And then that "movie" starts. Rourke struts into this room of Chinatown elders like he's John Wayne and starts going on and on, "Fuck you, fuck you. I'm tired of all this Chinese this, Chinese that. This is America." And then these young teenagers sitting across from us start going, "Right on, kick their butts." I started to feel scared. Can you believe that? "Right on Mickey, kick *their* asses!" I looked over at my friends. They all knew what was happening in that theater. As we walked out I could feel people staring at us. And the look in their eyes. I'm an American. Three fucking generations, *I'm an American.* And this goddamn movie comes along and makes me feel like I don't belong here. Like I'm the enemy. *I belong here.* I wanted to rip the whole goddamn fucking place up. Tear it all down. *(Silence. Vincent picks up Godzilla.)*

VINCENT.   Godzilla? Robinson Kan, a workshop production? *(Bradley nods.)* Well. "I never turn down a role." *(They both laugh. Vincent picks up script.*) Let's see what we have here. (*Dim to darkness.*)

End of Scene

Scene Five

"GODZILLA ... AAHK!"

Darkness. Godzilla-like theme music. High tension wires crackle across the projection screens.

VINCENT. *(V.O.)* I can't believe I let you talk me into this!
BRADLEY. *(V.O.)* Take it easy, take it easy.
VINCENT. *(V.O.)* I should have never let you talk me into this Asian American thing! And this costume...
BRADLEY. *(V.O. Interrupts.)* We're on! *(Bradley lit in pool of light D.R.. He plays a reporter out of the 50's. He wears a hat and holds one of those old-style announcer microphones.)* Good evening Mr. and Mrs. America and all the ships at sea. Flash! Godzilla!
VINCENT. *(On tape.)* AAHK!
REPORTER. A 1957 TOHO production. Filmed in Tokyo, to be distributed in Japan *AND* America. Starring Kehara Ken, the scientist who develops the anti-oxygen bomb that wipes out Godzilla...
GODZILLA. *(On tape.)* AAHK!
REPORTER. ... and Raymond Burr, an American actor who was so popular as Perry Mason that he just might be the drawing card needed to bring in those American audiences. Godzilla!...
GODZILLA. *(On tape.)* AAHK!
REPORTER. Rising, rising from the depths. In Japan it's released as *Gojira*. In America, it's Anglicized and marketed as *Godzilla!...* (*Vincent, dressed up in a Godzilla outfit, bursts through the projected high-tension wires as the projection screens turn to allow him to enter. Smoke and flashing lights.*)

GODZILLA. AAHK! *(During the following, Godzilla acts out what the Reporter is describing.)*

REPORTER. It breaks through the surface just off the shores of San Francisco. SPPLAASSHH!!! It's swum the entire Pacific Ocean underwater and is about to hyperventilate. It staggers onto the beach and collapses. It looks like a giant zucchini gone to seed. A huge capsized pickle with legs.

VICTOR. *(Struggling to get up.)* Bradley! Bradley, I'm stuck! *(Bradley helps Victor up.)*

REPORTER. 5 days later — refreshed and revived, it continues its trek inland. It takes the Great Highway up to Geary Boulevard, hangs a right on Gough and follows that sucker right onto the Bay Bridge. It pays no toll. Cars screech, children cry, mothers with babies scream. The men don't. They're "manly." Godzilla! ...

GODZILLA. AAHK! *(Godzilla strolls over to the Reporter/Bradley, takes the hat and mike and now he becomes the Reporter. Bradley, in turn, now becomes the Little Boy acting out what is said by Vincent.)*

REPORTER/GODZILLA/VINCENT. A little boy. A little boy watching TV. A little boy watching TV on Saturday night and it's "Creature Features" on Channel 2. Tonight the feature is "Godzilla..." *(Reporter momentarily becomes Godzilla.)* AAHK! *(Back to reporting.)* ...And a little boy watching, watching, has a hunger, a craving for a hero, for a symbol, for a secret agent to carry out his secret deeds ... Godzilla!

GODZILLA/LITTLE BOY. AAHK! *(Bradley grabs the hat and mike back and becomes the Reporter once again. Vincent as Godzilla acts out the blow by blow account.)*

REPORTER. ... In its anger it lashes out. It gouges out eyes of people who stare, rips out the tongues of people who taunt! Causes blackouts of old World War II movies! Godzilla!...

GODZILLA. AAHK!

REPORTER. It takes the 580 turn off and continues to head inland into the San Joaquin Valley. And there in the distance ... STOCKTON! Stockton, a small aggie town just south of Sacramento, population 120,000 and the home of a little boy. A little boy who knows, understands, and needs Godzilla...

GODZILLA.   AAHK!

REPORTER.   And who Godzilla...

GODZILLA.   AAHK!

REPORTER.   ... with his pea-sized brain, regards with supreme affection and would do anything the little boy asked it to do. And this is what the little boy asked... *(Bradley puts hat and mike aside and becomes the Little Boy.)*

BRADLEY/LITTLE BOY.   Godzilla, ya know Sammy Jones. She's this little fancy pants girl. She said she was watching this old war movie last night and that there was this female nurse — the *only* female in the whole entire army — and that a Japanese sniper shot her dead in the first 10 minutes of the movie. Then she said I was the enemy. And *then* she called me a "dirty Jap." *(Godzilla looks appalled, then angry.)* You know what to do. *(Godzilla turns, picks up a 'Sammy Jones' doll, looks down, and then dramatically stomps his foot down as if he were crushing a bug.)* OH BOY! OH BOY! *(End of Scene. Bradley and Vincent laughing. They had a good time together. They do a "right on" handshake. Godzilla-like music swells. Dim to darkness.)*

End of Act I

ACT II

INTERLUDE 4

Vincent lit in a pool of light. Body microphone. Visual projections.

VINCENT.   I have this dream. In this dream there is a man. And though this man is rich, successful, famous — he is unhappy, so very unhappy. He is unhappy because the love around him, the love in the hearts of those he cared for most, was beginning to shrivel and wither away. And this, in turn, made his own heart begin to grow in order to make up for the love that was disappearing around him. And the more the love in the hearts of those around him shriveled up, the bigger his own heart grew in order to make up for the growing emptiness that he now began to feel. So the love kept withering away and his heart kept growing bigger. Until one day there was so little love around him and his own heart so big — it burst into a thousand red petals that filled the sky and fell slowly, so very slowly, to the earth. And the people, his friends, the ones who had withheld their love, began to swallow the petals, these remains of the man's glorious heart as they fell from the sky. Hungrily, they fed. Greedily they swallowed. They pushed and shoved each other, gorging themselves on these petals because they felt then, they too, would become like the man. Rich, famous, beautiful, lonely... *(Vincent dims to darkness.)*

End of Interlude

Scene One

"WE WENT TO SEE THE MOVIE"

Bradley reading from a Shakespeare book. Rehearsing. Vincent coaching.

BRADLEY. Or art thou but
a dagger of the mind, a false creation,
Proceeding from the heat-oppressed —
(Vincent entering, correcting.)
VINCENT. Oppres-sed. Oppres-sed. *(Bradley, frustrated continues.)*
BRADLEY. ...heat oppres-sed brain?
I see thee yet, in form as palpable
As this which I now draw.
(Bradley draws a knife. Uncomfortable holding it.)
VINCENT. *(Overlapping towards end of Bradley's speech.)* ...which now I draw.
BRADLEY. ...now I draw, now I draw.
VINCENT. You should be elated you are doing Shakespeare. This is a great opportunity for you.
BRADLEY. *(Holding up a script.)* But this is Macbeth. I'm doing "Romeo and Juliet", Vincent — I'm doing Romeo.
VINCENT. *(Holding his book up.)* You must learn them all while you are still young. "Is this a dagger which I see before me, the handle toward my hand? Come, let me clutch thee." There is music to its language and you must know its rhythm so you can think clearly within its verse. I studied Shakespeare when I was younger. And I was — all modesty aside — the best Shakespearean actor in my class. But the only role I got was carrying a spear. And here you are with a gem of a role and you don't want to work. Come on, come on, let's hear it. *(Bradley puts his script aside and reads from his book.)*

BRADLEY.   Is this a dagger which I see before me,
The handle toward my hand? Come, let me clutch thee.
I have thee not and yet I see thee still
Art thou not, fatal vision, sensible
To feeling as to sight, or art thou but
A dagger of the mind, a false creation,
Proceeding from the heat-oppres-sed brain?
I see thee yet, in form as palpable
As this which now I draw.
VINCENT.   Thou marshal'st me the way that I was going —
(Bradley lowers his knife. Vincent notices.) Grip it. Hold it. You
must be able to imagine it, feel it. Know the experience
from the inside. Of course, you may not have wanted to kill
someone. You must know the feeling.
BRADLEY.   *(Overlapping after "kill someone".)* I'm having trouble
with this one, Vincent. I just can't. I can't. OK.
VINCENT.   This is ridiculous. You're too tense, way too tense.
Lie on the floor. *(Bradley resists.)* Lie on the floor. *(While
speaking Vincent lights up a cigarette. He needs a break and can do
this rote. Not paying attention to Bradley sprawled out on the ground,
trying out different shapes.)* Become a ... rock. You are a rock.
Find your shape. Are you big, small, flat, oblong? Keep look-
ing until you find your own particular shape. *(Bradley slowly
gets up into an upright position. Vincent puffing, doesn't notice.)*
Got it?
BRADLEY. Yeah.
VINCENT.   What do you feel? *(Vincent turns to see the stand-
ing Bradley.)*
BRADLEY.   Alive. Conscious. But there is no hunger, no
wanting. And no sense of time. It is now. Yes, that's it. Every-
thing is *now.*
VINCENT.   A rock that stands. With no appetite.
BRADLEY.   No, no really I know. This is what a rock feels.
VINCENT.   I have no reason not to believe.
BRADLEY.   I have been a rock before.
VINCENT.   Now I have a reason.
BRADLEY.   I have. On acid. LSD. The first time I dropped
acid I walked into a forest in the Santa Cruz mountains and

37

became a rock.

VINCENT. Why did you do this?

BRADLEY. I was in college.

VINCENT. Alright. Let's work with it. Since we finally have something. (*Putting out cigarette.*) Go with it Bradley. Relive the experience. Relive it moment by moment. Pebble by pebble. (*Suppressing giggle.*) I'm sorry.

BRADLEY. I am walking. There is a tightness I feel in the back of my neck — I guess it's the acid coming on. With each step I go deeper into the forest. And with each step I can feel the civilized part of me peeling away like an old skin. Whoo, my mind is beginning to cast aside whole concepts. God, the earth is breathing. I can feel it. It's like standing on someone's tummy. And this rock. This big, beautiful rock. Our consciousnesses are very similar. I do a Vulcan Mind-meld. (*Touching the rock.*) "I am waiting for nothing. I am expecting no one." (*Releases Vulcan Mind-meld.*) It is beautiful in its own rockness.

VINCENT. Good. OK, let us work with...

BRADLEY. I began walking again.

VINCENT. OK.

BRADLEY. Thoughts of great insight float in and out of my mind like pretty butterflies. Skin holds the body together. And the head holds the brain together. But what holds the mind together? *What holds the mind together?* I panic! I feel my mind beginning to drift away. There in nothing to hold my mind together. Soon bits and pieces of my consciousness will be scattered across the universe. I'll NEVER GRADUATE! What? What's this? Cows. 10, 20, 60, hundreds. Hundreds and hundreds of cows. Where did they come from? They spot me. They see that I am different. One cow steps forward. He is the leader. He wears a bell as a sign of his authority. He approaches me cautiously, studying me. This head cow nods in approval. He knows I am no longer a civilized human, but somehow different, like them. He turns and signals the others. They all begin to move towards me. Soon I am surrounded in a sea of friendly cows. Hello, hi — It's like old home week. Suddenly I hear a noise coming from far away. It tugs at something inside me. I turn to see where the noise is coming from. I see ... I recognize ... Jeffrey. My best friend. Calling my "name." I look at the cows. They are waiting to see what I will do. I look at Jeffrey, his voice ringing clearer and clearer, my name sounding more and more familiar. I look at the cows — They are beginning to turn away. Should I stay and run wild and free with the cows? Or, should I return to the dorms on campus? "HOWDY JEFFREY!" As I run back to see, the cows are once again pretending to be cows. They slowly lumber away, stupid and dumb. Moo, moo. *(Bradley notices Vincent staring at him.)* It's a true story.

VINCENT.   Cows?

BRADLEY.   Yes.

VINCENT.   Cows that have a double life? *(Bradley nods.)* The dumb facade they show to the outside world and their true cow selves that they show to one another when they are alone? Moo, moo? Well, back to the real world. Perhaps. Anyway, to the task at hand. The role you are playing. Let me rethink this. *(Holding book.)* "Is this a dagger which I see before me, the handle towards my hand? Come, let me clutch thee..."

BRADLEY.   *(Quietly.)* I killed someone.

VINCENT.   What?

BRADLEY.   I think I killed someone.

VINCENT.   Like in a person? A human being? *(Bradley nods.)* My God.

BRADLEY.   I'm not sure. I may have. But I'm not sure. It was stupid. So stupid. I was about 16. I used to hang around a lot with some Chinatown boys, gangs and that sort of thing. I was walking down Jackson Street with my girlfriend, we were going to see the movies, when these two guys — they must have been college students come to gawk at all the Chinese people — turned the corner. Well, as they walked passed, one of them looked at my girlfriend and said, "Hey, look at the yellow pussy." So I walked over to the one guy, "What did you say? What did you say?" He just laughed at me. So I pulled a knife and stabbed him. *(Shocked*

silence.)
VINCENT.   What happened then?
BRADLEY.   We went to see the movie. *(Pause.)* I don't know.
Sometimes it just builds up. The anger. *(Pause.)* That was over
10 years ago. I hope he's OK. I hope with my heart he's OK.
(Dim to darkness.)

End of Scene

INTERLUDE 5

*Darkness. Over house speakers we hear: "Un Bel Di Vedremo"
from* Madame Butterfly. *Vincent lit in pool of light. He re-
laxes at home, wearing a velvet bathrobe. He is seated, looking at himself in a mirror.*

VINCENT.   *(Repeated 2 times with different interpretations.)* "You
will cooperate or I will kill you." *(Pause.)* "You will cooperate
or I will kill you." I will take my moment. They expect me to
just read my lines and get the hell out of there, another
dumb North Vietnamese general. "You will cooperate or I
will kill you." Yes, I will take my moment. And I am not
going to let the director know. I won't tell Robert. I am just
going to do it. *(Pause. Smiling to himself.)* Yes, I will take my
moment. Vincent Chang is an actor. *(Vincent dims to darkness.
Music lowers in volume. Bradley lit in a pool of light.)*
BRADLEY.   *(On the phone.)* But why? I don't understand,
Jason. I thought we had an agreement, an understanding. I
know the series fell through, but I'm going to get other
roles. I'm a leading man. You told me so yourself. How
many young Asian American leading men are there? *(Beat.)*
I'm not *like* the rest of them. What? *(Listening.)* Yeah ... I've
heard of Snow Kwong Johnson. *(Bradley dims to darkness. Music
up. Vincent lit in a pool of light.)*
VINCENT.   Why do you keep threatening to do it? I hate that.
You know you won't do it. Besides I am not going to change

my mind. *(Pause.)* We can still see each other. *(Beat.)* As friends. *(His eyes follow someone out of the room. Music fades. Vincent dims. Music out. Bradley lit in a pool of light. He is talking to a friend.)*
BRADLEY. That's not true. Who said that about me? That's not true at all. What? I was an "ex-con?" I was a "hit-man" for the *what?* *(Pause. Butterfly's suicide aria in.)* Who told you this? Huh? Who told you this? *(Music swells and peaks as lights go down on Bradley.)*

End of Interlude

Scene Two

" ... HIT MAN FOR THE CHINESE MAFIA ..."

Vincent's apartment. Bradley has stormed in. Vincent is trying to put on his coat and pack a small duffle bag at the same time.

VINCENT. *(Putting things back into bag.)* I cannot talk now. I cannot. Now, *please.*
BRADLEY. *(Angry.)* Who else could have told them, Vincent? You're the only one who knows.
VINCENT. *(In a great hurry.)* Can't we talk about this later. I have to go somewhere. *(Pushing Bradley out of the way, continuing to pack.)*
BRADLEY. I told you in confidence. Haven't you heard of "confidentiality?" What do they call it, what do they call it — "privilege." Doctor-patient privilege. Lawyer-client privilege. *Actor-acting teacher privilege. (Vincent is all packed. Trying to get his coat on which has been dangling off his left shoulder.)*
VINCENT. I have to go Bradley. I have a very important appointment.
BRADLEY. *(Interrupts.)* Fuck your audition! What about *my* career? You told him, didn't you. Goddamn it. You told

41

everybody I was an ex-con, a hit-man for the *Chinese Mafia!* *(Pause.)* What if the casting agencies hear about it? Huh? Think they'll want to hire me?

VINCENT. *(Quietly.)* My friend is dying...

BRADLEY. *(Not hearing.)* What happens to my...

VINCENT. *(Interrupts.)* My friend is dying! *(Silence.)* He over-dosed. Took a whole bottle of pills. I have to go to the hospital. Now, get out of my way, Bradley. *(Pushing a stunned Bradley aside.)* There are some things in this world more important than *your* career ... What has happened to you Bradley? What the hell has happened to you?

BRADLEY. *(Quietly.)* I just wanted to know. That's all. If you told him. I haven't gotten a call lately and I thought you know... *(Pause. Vincent feels badly about his remarks.)*

VINCENT. Look. I am sorry...

BRADLEY. You better go Vincent, your friend...

VINCENT. *(Starts to leave, stops.)* He always does this. My friend is just ... lonely. He wants me to come running.

BRADLEY. You said he took a whole bottle of sleeping pills?

VINCENT. Last time it was a whole bottle of laxatives. One week in the hospital. He was so happy. He lost 15 pounds. *(Pause.)* Maybe I did. *(Bradley doesn't follow his comment.)* Mention it. About what happened in Chinatown. Just to a few people. I just never had someone tell me they killed...

BRADLEY. *(Overlapping.)* He's probably OK, now. I'm sure the guy's fine.

VINCENT. ...someone before. I had to tell somebody. And I never said you were a hit-man for the Chinese Mafia, or whatever... *(Pause.)* I am sorry, Bradley. Remember? *(Taps his nose.)* Dr. Lao? I have to go. The nurses may need some help with the bed pans. *(Notices Bradley.)* We all go through these periods when the phone does not ring. I, too, have had them. Of course, far and few between, but I, too. Try some "ochazuke" with some "umeboshi" — it's on the stove. My mother used to make me eat it when I was upset. Soothes the nerves. *(Vincent turns to exit.)*

BRADLEY. Vincent? I was going to kick your ass. I was.

(Vincent stops. Stares at Bradley.) I just sit in my room, waiting for the phone to ring. Why won't the phone ring, Vincent? Huh? Why won't the goddamn phone ring? *(Dim to darkness.)*

End of Scene

INTERLUDE 6

Darkness. We hear Bradley's voice. Gradually lights are brought up as he speaks. Up stage area, lit in a pool of light. Body microphone. Visual projections.

BRADLEY.   I have this dream. In this dream, I'm lying on a park bench. I wear only a very ragged black overcoat. Then, I fall asleep. My mouth wide open. It is a kind of perfect sleep. No hunger, no desire ... no dreams. My heart stops beating. The blood comes to rest in my veins. *(Noticing.)* It's quite pleasureful. The whispering of warm breezes through my hair. Big, colorful maple leaves of red and orange that flutter down and cover my eyes like coins. Ahh ... What's this? 2 dark clouds circling high above. Now they swoop down, down, towards my sleeping corpse. I see what they are. Two magnificent vultures. I think of something to offer. "Here, here, take my fingers. Yes, yes ... don't be afraid. Here, take the rest of my hand." That should be enough. No. They want more ... They've jumped on my chest. They're beginning to rip me open. It feels ... so ... so ... *(Dim to darkness.)*

End of Interlude

Scene Three

"I SEE MYSELF 35 YEARS AGO"

Thunder. Bradley seated on a bench in a small outdoor shelter. Raining. Umbrella on ground. Vincent runs to the shelter holding 2 cups of hot coffee.

VINCENT.   *(Hands coffee to Bradley.)*   Black, right?   *(Bradley nods, takes coffee. Sips, watches rain.)*
BRADLEY.   I finally got a call. I just came from an audition. It was for one of those evening soaps, everybody was there. Butler gig, glorified extra. I didn't get the role. I walked outside and I started crying. And I was crying, not because of the humiliation. But because, *I wanted the role.* I keep thinking, if I got it, the part, could I go through with it? I mean, actually show up and do that stuff?
VINCENT.   When you walk on that set and there is all that expectation from everyone — the director, the writer, the other actors to be that way, it is so ... I was watching TV last week. They had on this story about Martin Luther King. He was picked up by some night riders. Drove him to the outskirts of town, dragged him out of the car and surrounded him. And that night he felt something inside he never felt before — impotent, like the slave, willing to go along, almost wanting to comply. After that, he realized he had to fight not only the white man on the outside, but that feeling, the slave inside of him. It is so easy to slip into being the "ching-chong-chinaman." *(Vincent looks at Bradley, knowingly.)* Moo, moo.
BRADLEY.   It's still raining pretty hard. I felt kind a bad about last time. That's why I called you up. Your friend OK? *(Vincent nods. Pause.)*

44

VINCENT.   I love the rain. It is like meditating. It seems to quiet all the distractions around you so you can better hear the voice of your own heart. The heart. A mysterious thing. Kind. Cruel. At times you would like to rip it out. It feels too much, gives you too much pain. And other times — aah, the ecstasy. You wish it were a huge golden peach so that everyone might taste of its sweetness. *(Pause. Thinks.)* It is also like a mirror. Yes, a mirror. And if one is brave enough to gaze into it, in it is reflected the truth of what we really are. Not as we would like to be, or as we would like the world to see us. But as we truly are. *(Vincent looks at Bradley intently.)* Would you like to know what I see? *(Bradley motions to himself, questioningly. Vincent nods.)*
BRADLEY.   That's OK, I'd rather you didn't tell me. An egomaniac, right? A selfish, arrogant, insecure actor.
VINCENT.   No, no, quite the contrary. I see a sensitive, shy and compassionate soul. *(Pause.)*   And I see a driven, ambitious, self-centered asshole. In other words, I see myself 35 years ago. *(They laugh quietly.)*
BRADLEY.   I know this sounds kind of silly. I've never told anyone. You know how everyone has these secret goals. You know what mine were? Obie, Oscar, Tony. OOT. *(They quietly laugh.)*
VINCENT.   I was so cocky after my Oscar nomination. No more of those lousy chinaman's parts for me anymore. This was my ticket out of there. Hell, I might even call my own shots. My agent kept warning me though. " 'Vincent, you're an oriental actor. It's different for you.' I said, 'No way. Not anymore. From now on only good roles are coming my way.'
BRADLEY.   Did the offers for good roles come in?
VINCENT.   No." I have this dream. I am standing in the * middle of a room with all these people staring at me. At first I think they are friendly towards me. Then I think, no, they

---

* Dialogue based on a scene from the film, *Yuki Shimoda* by John Esaki and Amy Kato.

are evil people out to get me. Then suddenly again, I think this is exactly where I want to be, it feels wonderful. Then I am seized with a strange fear and I feel I must get the hell out of there. A spotlight flashes on me. I am disoriented. Someone hands me a script. *(Vincent glances at the lines.)* "Why do I have to do this?" Then this warm, soothing voice says, "Is there a problem Vincent? All we want you to do is fuck yourself. Take all the time you want. We'll get the most expensive lubricant if you need. Vincent, is there a problem? We hear Sly Stallone's doing it, so it must be OK. OK?" "Read the lines this way." *(Pause.)* I know what is going on, Bradley. I am not stupid. I know what I am doing. That is the problem. *(They sip their drinks in silence. Watch the rain.)*

BRADLEY. Maybe you should call Gumbo's, that bar in San Francisco. Right now. Come on, let's be crazy!

VINCENT. What? And find out that my beautiful memory of Jade Wing has turned into — what did you say? A grouchy old bitch? No. I could not bear to kill any more of my dreams.

BRADLEY. That was probably just the bartender. Jade is probably rich, still beautiful, living in some expensive home in Pacific Heights, wondering this very instant, "What ever happened to Shig Nakada?" *(Vincent sadly shakes his head.)*

VINCENT. We were married. Jade and I. No one ever knew that. Just us. We were so young. *(Pause.)* She left me one night. Never saw her again. I don't blame her. She caught me in bed with someone.

BRADLEY. Vincent.

VINCENT. Actually, she did not mind the idea of me playing around. Or rather she minded but she could live with it. What she could not stomach was who I was playing around with. *(Pause.)* Well. It is getting late. And the rain seems to have finally abated. *(Both get up.)* Bradley? Would you like to come over to my place? For a drink? *(Awkward pause.)*

BRADLEY. No, Vincent. No, I can't.

VINCENT. Right. Well. Good night. *(Pause.)*

BRADLEY. It's OK. *(Vincent doesn't follow.)* It's OK, Vincent. It doesn't matter to me.

VINCENT.   I do not know what you are talking about.
BRADLEY.   It doesn't matter, Vincent. People don't care
nowadays.
VINCENT.   I do not know what you are talking about Bradley. I do not. It is late. Good-bye.
BRADLEY.   Good night, Vincent. *(Bradley sadly watches Vincent
exit. Dim to darkness.)*

End of Scene

INTERLUDE 7

Bradley lit in pool of light, sitting.

BRADLEY.   *(Bragging.)*   They want me to play this Chinese
waiter. I'll go, OK, take a look. I get there and look at the
script. Jesus. I read the lines straight. No accent, no nothing.
They say, "No, no, we need an accent." You know, THE accent. I told my agent — What? No, I quit them — if they
pay me twice the amount of the offer, OK. I'll do it anyway
they want. Otherwise forget it. They paid it. The dumb shits.
They paid it. *(Laughing smugly.)* On top of it, they liked me.
Yeah, they liked me. *(Cross fade to an empty pool of light. The
aria from* Madame Butterfly *softly underscoring this scene. Vincent
enters dancing. He is wearing headphones with a walkman and is
practicing one of his old routines. Gradually the TV light and sound
are brought up. We hear the Sergeant Moto monologue. Vincent stops
dancing, takes off headphones and watches the TV light. Upset. Reaches
for the phone and dials for his agent.)*
VINCENT'S VOICE ON TV.   You stupid American G.I. I know
you try and escape. You think you can pull my leg. I speakee
your language. I graduate UCLA, Class of 34. I drive big,
American car with big chested American blond sitting next to
— Heh? No, no, not "dirty floor." Floor clean. Class of 34.
No, no, not "dirty floor." Floor clean, just clean this morning.
34. No, no, not "dirty floor." Listen carefully. Watch my
lips. 34. 34! 34!!! What is wrong with you? You sickee in the

47

head? What the hell is wrong with you? Why can't you hear what I 'm saying? Why can't you see me as I really am? *(Dim to darkness on Vincent dialing the phone.)*

End of Interlude

Scene Four

"AHHH ... THE NORTH STAR"

Six months later. Party at the same home in the Hollywood Hills. Balcony. Night. Vincent sips on a drink and stares into the night sky. Bradley appears. Walks over and stands beside him. They watch stars in silence.

VINCENT. *(Notices Bradley's drink.)* Tanins are bad for your complexion. *(They both laugh, clink glasses and sip.)* It's been a while. What, 6 months or so? I tried calling your service.

BRADLEY. It's been a little hectic. My girlfriend moved down from San Francisco.

VINCENT. Oh, I didn't know. I've been seeing more of my friend ... Kenneth.

BRADLEY. Ahh, Kenneth. *(Pause.)*

VINCENT. You look good. Different. *(Looking closer at Bradley.)* What is it? Your hair? Your nose?

BRADLEY. Oh, yeah. I was having a sinus problem, so I thought, you know, while they were doing that they might as well...

VINCENT. Ahhh. It looks good.

BRADLEY. You look good.

VINCENT. Always.

BRADLEY. God. The night air. Ahhh. It was getting a bit stuffy in there.

VINCENT. I thought you liked being around Asians.

BRADLEY. Yeah, but not a whole room full of them. *(They both laugh.)* No way I can protect my back side. *(Mimes jabbing a knife.)*

48

VINCENT.   Ahhh.   *(Awkward pause. Bradley embarrassed that Vincent didn't laugh at the knife joke. Vincent looks up at the night sky.)* Pointing The Big Dipper. Follow the two stars that form its lip and...
BRADLEY.   The North Star.
VINCENT.   Voila! You will never be lost, my dear friend. Never. *(Silence. They sip their drinks.)* Something interesting happened to me last week. I was offered a very well paying job in that new film everyone is talking about, *Angry Yellow Planet.*
BRADLEY.   I read for that movie, too.
VINCENT.   Playing "Yang, the Evil One."
BRADLEY.   Yang! Hah! I read for the part of Yang's number one son. We could be father and son. Might be interesting.
VINCENT.   Yes.
BRADLEY.   Then again it might not. *(Both laugh at the old joke.)* You know what, Vincent? You won't believe this...
VINCENT.   I turned it down. *(No response.)* I just could not do it. Not this time. *(Pause.)* It feels ... It feels good. Almost. I turned it down to be in Emily Sakoda's new film. It is about a Japanese American family living in Sacramento before the war. Just like my childhood. 16mm, everyone deferring pay. And my role, it's wonderful. I get to play my father. *(Mimics father.)* "Urusai, yo!" That. It's my father. And this ... "So - ka?" I mean, it's so damn exciting, Bradley. I had forgotten what it feels like. What it is supposed to feel like. Do you know what I mean?
BRADLEY.   I took it. *(Vincent doesn't follow.)* I took *it.* The role.
VINCENT.   Oh...
BRADLEY.   I took the role of Yang's number one son. He's half Chinese and half rock.
VINCENT.   I see.
BRADLEY.   It's a science fiction movie.
VINCENT.   Ahhh.
BRADLEY.   I figure once I get there I can change it. I can sit down with the producers and writers and explain the situation. Look, if I don't take it then what happens? Some other jerk takes it and plays it like some goddamned

geek.

VINCENT. Yes. Well.

BRADLEY. I'll sit down and convince them to change it. I will. Even if it's a bit. Just a small change, it's still something. And, even if they don't change it, they'll at least know how we feel and next time, maybe next time...

VINCENT. Yes.

BRADLEY. And in that sense. In a small way. It's a victory. Yes, a victory. *(Pause.)* Remember this? *(Sings.)* Tea cakes and moon songs... *(They both laugh. Pause. Bradley looks at Vincent.)* Moo, moo. *(Muttering to himself.)* Fucking cows.

VINCENT. Remember this? *(Starts Sergeant Moto monologue with the same stereotypic reading as in the opening Interlude, but quickly loses accent. And, ultimately, performs with great passion.)* You stupid American G.I. I know you try to escape. You think you can pull my leg. I speakee your language. *(Accent fading.)* I graduated from UCLA, the Class of 1934. I had this big car... *(Accent gone.)* What? No, no, not "dirty floor." The floor is clean. Class of 34. No, no, not "dirty floor." I had it cleaned this morning. How many times do I have to tell you. 34. Class of 34. No, no, not "dirty floor." Listen carefully and watch my lips. 34. 34! 34!! What is wrong with you? What the hell is wrong with you? I graduated from the University of California right here in Los Angeles. I was born and raised in the San Joaquin Valley and spent my entire life growing up in California. Why can't you hear what I'm saying? Why can't you see me as I really am? *(Vincent stops. Bradley is truly moved. Bradley quietly applauds his performance. They smile at each other. They turn to look out at the night sky. They are now lit in a pool of light. Bradely points to the lip of the Big Dipper and moving his hand traces a path to the North Star.)* Ahhh. The North Star. *(Vincent and Bradley begin a slow fade to black. At the same time, the theater is again filled with a vast array of stars. The music swells in volume. As Vincent and Bradley fade to black, the stars hold for a beat. Then, surge in brightness for a moment. Then, blackout. Screen: "THE END". Screen darkens.)*

END OF PLAY

PROPERTY PLOT

Off, Down Right

Plastic train
Cordless microphone with stand
Award
2 cordless telephones
Beer bottle (open, with water 1/2 full)
Cowboy hat
Reporter/Godzilla hat
Old-style announcer's microphone
'Sammy Jones' doll
Black motorcycle jacket
Sides of *The Wash*
Moto outfit: hat
               gloves
               glasses
               gun
               riding crop
Hairbrush
Ashcan

Off, Right Portal

Ashcan with water
Tea towel
Plastic cup of club soda
Red t-shirt
Black suit jacket
2 cassette tapes in cases
Duffel bag with: gray sweatjacket
                    pack of gum
                    small pad with pencil in ring
                    comb
                    eyedrops

                        miscellaneous items
                        men's ring in outside pocket
                        Godzilla toy
Hairbrush
Check tray with check

Off, Up Right

Lawn chair with: footrest, attached
                    padding, attached
                    outdoor ashtray, on seat
1 iron chair
Canvas bag with: bag of chocolates
                    contact lens solution
                    mini-Walkman with cassette
                    1 pair of socks
                    a crystal
                    comb
                    pen/pencil
                    thermos of warm ginger tea
                    bound script
                    notepad
                    empty cassette case

Kitchen

Indoor ashtray
Martini glass
Generic bar drink glass
2 capuccino cups
2 wine glasses
Drink mixtures: red wine
                    club soda
                    coffee
                    Pepsi
                    tea (in thermos)

Olives
Ice
Cigarettes
Lighter or matches

Off, Down Left

Camera set with flash
Stereotypic glasses
Stack of goodies: pajamas
                   slippers
                   shaving kit
                   toothbrush
                   toothpaste

Off, Left Portal

Sunglasses
Cordless phone
Iron chair with script of *The Wash*

Off, Up Left

Ashcan with water
Tea towel
Glass of red wine
'Sammy Jones' doll
Hairbrush

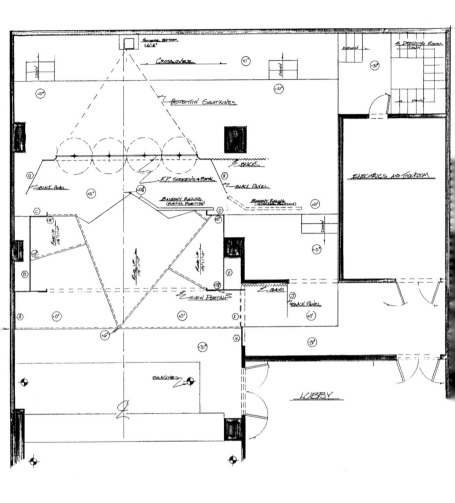

SCENE DESIGN

"YANKEE DAWG YOU DIE"
(Designed by Kent Dorsey for the
Playwrights Horizons' production.)

NOTES
(Use this space to make notes for your production)

NOTES
(Use this space to make notes for your production)